Brittney Griner

By Jon M. Fishman

AMAZING ATHLETES

Lerner Publications Company • Minneapolis

Brittney Griner *(center)* powers to the hoop against the Chicago Sky.

INSTANT IMPACT

Brittney Griner's first game in the Women's National Basketball Association (WNBA) was not going well. On May 27, 2013, the Phoenix Mercury were losing to the Chicago Sky. The game had just started. But Brittney was eager to show the fans what she could do.

Brittney plays **center** for the Mercury. The team had chosen her with the first pick in the **draft** just one month before. Brittney had been one of the best players in college basketball history. Could she be just as good in the WNBA?

Brittney was raised in the city of Houston, Texas.

DADDY'S GIRL

Brittney was born on October 18, 1990, in Houston, Texas. Her middle name is Yevette. Brittney's parents are Ray and Sandra. Ray worked as a police officer in Houston for many years. Sandra stayed home to take care of the family. Brittney is the youngest of four children. She has an older brother and two older sisters.

Brittney didn't like to do the things her brother and sisters did. They spent time talking on the phone or watching TV. Brittney liked to be outside. She played in her yard and climbed trees. She also worked on the family cars with her father in the evenings. "I was a daddy's girl and loved being out there changing oil and tires with him," she said. Brittney can still help her friends if they have car trouble.

Ray had played football in high school. But Sandra didn't like sports. She preferred to stay inside and make blankets and watch cooking shows on TV. Brittney took after her father.

Brittney takes a shot for Nimitz High School.

GROWING INTO THE GAME

The girls' basketball team at Nimitz had never had a player like Brittney before. At 15 years old, she already stood 6 feet tall. She was also very athletic. Brittney had a lot to learn about basketball. But she caught on fast. She was named one of the best players in the **district** at the end of the season.

By the start of the 2006–2007 season, Brittney had shot up another 6 inches. She used her height to her advantage. She averaged 23 points per game as a sophomore. She also racked up 10.5 rebounds and 6.1 **blocked shots** per game. Brittney's most exciting play as a sophomore came against nearby Northbrook High School.

With her height and great skill, Brittney makes dunking the ball look easy.

Brittney lifts up her Naismith Trophy.

FIRST PICK

Brittney won a slew of awards after the 2011–2012 season. The Atlanta Tipoff Club presented her with the Naismith Trophy. This award goes to the top college player in women's basketball. She won the trophy again after the 2012–2013 season. Although Baylor couldn't repeat their championship run, Brittney's senior season marked the end of a great college career. She still holds the records for most blocks (748) and most dunks (18) in women's college history.

On April 16, 2013, Brittney attended the WNBA draft. No one was surprised when the Phoenix Mercury chose her with the first pick. "It's a dream come true," Brittney said. "I'm like a little kid in Disney World the first time meeting all the characters."

Brittney with Mercury head coach Corey Gaines *(left)* and President Amber Cox *(right)* at the 2013 draft.